Nasty Nate's
Pirate Adventure

Marcia Vaughan
Illustrated by Chris Smedley
and Deborah Allwright

OXFORD

Chapter 1 – Believe it or not!

It happened so fast Nate could hardly believe it.

One minute he was sitting at his computer playing a new game. It was called **PIRATE TREASURE.**

The next minute he felt dizzy. The computer, the desk and his room spun round and round. He felt himself being lifted up and ... pulled into the game!

PIRATE TREASURE

LIVES

Suddenly, Nate was face to face
with a crew of real pirates! They did
not look happy to find him on their ship.

"Blimey!" said a pirate with bad breath.
"What have we here?"

"A stowaway!" cried a pirate with a peg leg.

"A spy!" cried a pirate with a silver hook.

"Aarrr! Let's feed this landlubber to the
sharks," added a pirate with no teeth.

Before Nate could cry for help the pirates
picked him up and dragged him to the rail.

"On the count of three, we drop him in
the drink," said the peg-legged pirate. "One …
two … uh … What comes after two?"

"Three!" yelled the other pirates.

The pirates were just about to let go when a pirate with a large hat and gold eye patch called out, "Stop right there lads! 'Tis only a boy. I orders you to put him down."

"Aye, aye, Captain Patch," the crew grumbled. They dropped Nate – kerplunk – on the dirty deck.

"What be your name, matey?" Captain Patch asked.

"Nate, sir," Nate replied.

Captain Patch pulled Nate to his feet. "Well, you're a pirate now, me lad, so I'll be calling you Nasty Nate. We're off to find buried treasure and we be needing a cabin boy."

Nate was given a red bandana for his head. He was also given a brush for scrubbing the deck. "I'm a real pirate," Nate said to himself and grinned.

Chapter 2 – Walking the plank

Nasty Nate liked being a pirate. He got to sleep in a hammock. He got to eat pirate grub. He got to swing from the ropes. He never had to bathe, wash his clothes or brush his teeth. The crew wasn't very friendly but Captain Patch always gave him a smile.

BARNACLE STEW

One morning, Nate was scrubbing the deck near the galley. He heard the crew whispering.

"I say we steal the captain's map," said Peg-leg Pete.

"Then we make him walk the plank," said Hook-finger Fred.

"Then we don't have to give him half the treasure," said Toothless Ted.

"Ooh aarrr!" cried Bad-breath Bill. "Let's go!"

Nate ran to warn Captain Patch. The crew saw him and pushed him aside. They pointed their broom handles at the captain. They made him hand over the treasure map hidden in his right boot.

"Now, it's time to walk the plank," said Bad-breath Bill.

Captain Patch stood on the plank. "You scurvy sea dogs be making a mistake. You'll never find the treasure without me."

Hook-finger Fred gave him a push. Together Captain Patch and Nasty Nate fell into the sea.

"Captain Patch!" spluttered Nate in surprise. "Why did you let them do that?"

Captain Patch swam to Nate. He helped him stay afloat. "Don't worry, matey, it's all part of my plan. We had to get away from those rotten rascals."

"But we'll drown!" cried Nate.

"No we won't, me hearty," the captain said. "A pirate captain always has a plan. I tied a lifeboat to the stern of the ship. Look! *And* I gave those no-good pirates a fake map. It will lead them to nothing but … well, nothing! The real treasure is buried on that island. All we've got to do is reach it. Nothing can go wrong now."

Nasty Nate was about to agree. Then he saw something in the water. It made his blood run cold.

"Captain!" Nate cried. "What's that?"

The tall, pointed fin cut through the water like a knife. It was coming right at them.

"Shiver me timbers!" cried Captain Patch in alarm. "It's a shark! Swim fer yer life!"

Chapter 3 – Hunting for treasure

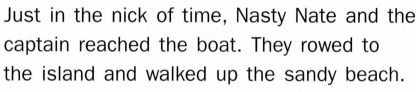

Just in the nick of time, Nasty Nate and the captain reached the boat. They rowed to the island and walked up the sandy beach.

Captain Patch pulled a piece of soggy paper from his left boot. He gave it to Nate.

"That there's the *real* map," Captain Patch said. "The only thing is, it's not a drawing … it's words. Blast the barnacles off my behind if I don't know how to read. That's why I needed a smart boy like you in my crew."

Nate looked at the map and read the clues aloud:

Up on the hill, by the old parrot's nest
Take ten paces south and four paces west.
Stop, take your shovel, and dig, dig, DIG!
Then, if you like, you can dance a silly jig!

"I'm sorry, Captain Patch," said Nate. "The clues don't mean a thing to me."

The captain threw his arms in the air. "Arr-har, Nate me lad. The old parrot's nest is up there, in that tree at the centre of the island. That must be where the treasure is buried!"

Nasty Nate and the captain hurried to the old parrot's nest. Nate looked up at the sky.

"That must be west," he said, pointing to the setting sun.

They took ten paces south and then four paces west.

Then Captain Patch took his shovel and started to dig.

Moments later, Captain Patch pulled out a big chest. He opened the lid. Inside were hundreds of gold coins!

"Hoo-har! We be rich!" cheered the captain. He danced a silly jig. "Go ahead, matey. Fill yer pockets to the top."

With a grin, Nate reached out to grab a handful of coins. Just as he touched them, he felt dizzy. Captain Patch, the island and the treasure chest spun round and round. He felt himself being lifted up and ... pulled out of the game!

It happened so fast Nate could hardly believe it.

He was sitting at his computer. On the screen Captain Patch smiled and gave him a wink. Then the game ended. The screen went dark.

"What a cool game!" said Nate. "It was so real!"

Then he put his hand in his pocket and pulled something out.

"Well, shiver me timbers!" cried Nate. He looked down and there in his hand sat a shiny gold coin!

Meanwhile, will that no-good pirate crew ever realise the map they have is fake?

The map says the treasure is just around the bend, mateys!

Ahoy, Yeti. Have ya seen any treasure?

Dig, mateys, dig!

ROAR!

Aargh, this place be looking familiar.

Ooh, look at the pretty fish!

Where's the lifeboat?

Look at the yummy pirates!